The Wayfarer

SHAILENDRA SHARMA

ISBN: 1470028824
ISBN 13: 9781470028824

Translated by Bhushan Jawlekar and Prachi Jawlekar

In 1992-1993, when I left home and was looking for a place in Brij, from October 1992 to June 1993 I saw a lot and endured a lot. In those days my younger sister Devahuti, who was also roaming around with me, wrote something. In reaction to that, some poems came from within during the three days of Holi (festival of colors in India); they are in front of you in the form of *The Wayfarer.*

Do you know what expression is?
Can you explain what expression is?
Are you able to conceive what expression is?
How does one express what springs from within?
Don't you know? Then listen

One, who breaks in to expression,
Takes the pen of his feelings
Dips it in to his heart
Making his blood the ink
Writes a few lines on life

That's what expression is
Yes, that's what it is
Writing, it is not
Expression it is,
That is written with the ink of blood
With the pen of feelings
On the pages of life

O wayfarer, on the path of life,
Do you see the dust strewn on the path of life?
Here are those who came before you
These are their marks
On this, appear the footprints of those who stride ahead
Worry not that you would not make it
Do not lose heart that the goal is far away
Remember, with every step you take
That much closer your goal it makes
O wayfarer, stop not, keep walking
For if you, the dust shall you meet

These are those who had started walking
But tired, they stopped, you keep walking
Keep walking leaving your footprints
Advance, keep walking, and keep walking
Then you would realize that the path itself has become your goal
Stop not, stop not
Many would stop you with calls from behind
But you keep walking
For if you turn, you shall stumble
You will fall in this same dust
Keep your sight on the horizon
To touch it is your goal
Wherever you meet your goal
Take it that you shall meet yourself

Walking on the path of life
Do not forget those in your haste
Who became the dust, for they stopped
Don't you pity this dust
Don't you consider yourself its superior
For the weary who fell, became the dust
They did not succeed in reaching there
For which they had started once
They will inspire you
Stop you will not, thanks to the experience of those
Who became the dust falling somewhere
Forget not the dust strewn on the path of life
For this dust shall save you from the thorns
Yes, but for this dust who knows how many thorns would prick you
This shall make your path serene

While walking, stop if you can
Pick it up, yes this same dust
And smear it on your forehead
As it is this outcome which shall stop you from stopping
And will take you there
To reach where you had started walking
And if you can not reach your goal
Even then do not lose heart
Meet the dust strewn on the path
And become dust yourself
By becoming the dust you might be happy
For by becoming the dust you have succeeded
In paving the way for those who would overtake you

Walking on this path you shall meet many
Who stumbled and fell
Seeing them, compassion will arise in your heart
Which is only natural
But beware; do not stop to support them
If you stop to support them, then you halt
Know that those stumbled shall hold you so much
That you would not possibly advance
You will stumble yourself and you will remain
There among those who stumbled
Compassion traps the man in the bondage of giving support
And if you are bound in there
Then walk you would not be able to
You shall remain there under the pretext of giving support

Look, when you see those who stumbled and fell
Then you give them the support of inspiration
Seeing one fallen, ask him to rise
Tell him he can walk and you go ahead
For this will be the support
Out of your compassion
The stumbled and fallen will get the support of inspiration
Seeing you, the fallen shall rise
With all his strength
And will start walking with his tired, heavy feet
You only become his inspiration
O wayfarer, you only keep walking

You started
Accepting the challenge of knowing your wherewithal
Of knowing your limits
You walked and walked
To touch the horizon of your wherewithal
You walked and walked
You lived your life walking and walking
But stopped you not; only walked

When you reach the horizon
When you succeed in touching it
Then you turn around and see
You will find other wayfarers walking
Following the footprints that you left
On the sand of time strewn on the path of life
Walking on the path of life
Inspired by you, yes by you
Watching your footprints
They must be picturing
How would he be who left these footprints
These footprints that inspire those who walk
How would that wayfarer be?
Not here now, he must have touched his horizon
But is being remembered for
What he left behind

O wayfarer, until you touch your horizon
You keep walking
To become the inspiration of those who walk
You just walk on

Be not fearful while walking on the path
And be not afraid of what would happen ahead
Would you be able to walk or not?
Would you stumble, would you reach your horizon?
Be not afraid on the path of life
Holding the finger of life and with inspiration in heart
You walk; keep walking
Walking and walking you will know that the path of life
Does not let those become careless
Who walk on it
Who walk along it with inspiration in their hearts
Who set out to touch the horizon
With the treasure of breaths and the reserves of life

This is the path of life
That tires the one who walks
Carrying inspiration in heart for walking on it
He loses himself in older memories
Loses the sight of horizon
Then a stumble on this path
Warns him to go wakefully ahead

Do not be lost in memories
You have to go ahead, much ahead
O wayfarer, taking the reserves of life
To touch the horizon, you just walk on

While walking on the path of life
Escaping from the bonds of compassion
Getting inspired from the dust strewn on the path
Smearing that dust on the forehead
When you advance to touch your horizon
Takings the reserves of life
When the inspiration in your heart will show you the way
You would be walking in your own rhythm
Keeping your sight on that horizon
Which you had set out to touch
You are walking and you will keep walking to touch it

While walking on this path you will find
Sitting unworried on the side of path
Someone, who is not part of the strewn dust
Someone who did not stumble
One who is not desperate to touch the horizon
O wayfarer, if you find someone so unworried
Then stop for a few moments
He must be the one whose footprints inspired you
To keep walking
He would have come back after touching the horizon
Perhaps to tell you something
You stop by him
And absorb his experience
But remember; take it with your heart spread open
He will inspire you to touch the horizon
His experiences will be the reserves for your journey
And perhaps your goal too
You take them in your heart and advance
And then before touching the horizon
You stop not; just walk on

When the eagerness to touch the horizon
Will inspire you to walk
And when you will find the path in front of you stretched to
infinity
Then for not having walked ever
Your heart will tremble, your mind will say to you
Stay back, where are you going?
Where will you find this pleasant warmth of relations?
Those you consider your own
And those who have brought you to existence
Will you be able to break the pleasant bond of their proximity?
You will find it hard to break
When you find it hard, leave everything and walk
And look once, only once, towards the horizon
Where you will see the path meeting infinity
You take inspiration from it
And just walk ahead
While walking you will be pulled back
By the pleasant warmth of the nest
But taking the reserves of life
And a little bit of courage in heart
Confront a few storms and harsh gales
That you encounter full of dust on the way
You only keep the horizon in sight
Walk, stop not, and walk on

Leaving the pleasant warmth of your nest
Leaving the lure of kinfolk
When you will walk on that unknown path
With a trembling heart and dream in your eyes
You will find a crowd on the path
That will seem nearer and dearer
When you see them blocking the path, you be forewarned
Know that it is a crowd of those
Who are afraid of walking
And are envious of those who walk
They would stop you; they would want you to be one of them
But don't you look away from horizon
Don't you listen to the howls of crowd
They will frighten you
And when they can not, they will condemn you
But you do not stop near them
With your trembling heart
And the reserves of life in your hand
Only watching the horizon
On that path that appears to meet infinity
You walk, stop not and walk on

Keep the sight on horizon
While walking on the path
That will take you to infinity

With a trembling heart
And with an inspiration from someone's footprints
With the fretfulness of touching the horizon
Leaving that crowd behind
And leaving that pleasant warmth of the nest
When you move ahead, you will find
That no one was distressed by your walking
That no one shed a tear
And the one who does not want to go down that path
You are not for him anymore
Do not forget that crowd memory is short
When it can not stop those who walk
When it can not make them its own
Then it stops worrying about them
And cowers in itself
It waits for someone else
Who will walk with inspiration from your footprints
You only walk, stop not, walk
Walking and walking you will reach the horizon
And when you feel you are about to touch the horizon
You will find only yourself there
And you will welcome you yourself
But until then stop not
With dream in your eyes you walk on

Walking and walking on the path when your legs tire
When you feel it is difficult to walk now
And you feel you could stop for a moment
You could have had someone who could have shored you up
A little
Just a little
But beware, do not stop; do not look for support
For if you search it, you would not be able to walk
You will fall there and become the dust
If you stop and look for support
O wayfarer, when you feel someone should shore you up
Look at the horizon
And give support to yourself all by yourself
And only walk on
Do not forget, always remember
That there is no one better than you
To support yourself
You give it, when your legs tire,
The support to yourself
And with that you walk on
To touch the horizon, you walk on

Do you see this path of life
On which you have to walk with the reserves of life
Leaving the dear one and that crowd that seems your own
With a little courage in your heart
With a dream of touching the horizon in your eyes
You walk, but remember
Walk on it with caution
The path is slippery
With the mud of hope and despair
You will also find blind turns
Duck them
O wayfarer, don't you get lost in these blind alleys
You keep walking supporting yourself
With the treasure of inspiration
To touch your own frontiers
On that path, O wayfarer, you only keep walking
If you ever fall on it, then just remember
No one will shore you up,
Neither your dear ones nor the crowd that seems your own
By falling you will only entertain them
You will have to support yourself
Even if you fall, even if you are injured
Console yourself
That falls he who walks to touch the horizon
Falling makes him mature
And fills him with resolve
To keep walking on the path
To touch his own frontier
O wayfarer! You remember this
And you walk ahead
Do not stop, you just walk on

You are walking to touch the horizon
Thinking you will know yourself
By knowing your frontiers
You will someday become limitless

When you reach yourself, touching the horizon
Then you turn around and look towards us
We could not walk on this difficult path
We remained as dust somewhere
That seemingly our own crowd overwhelmed us
Which could not stop you
You remember us
Those who could not walk
We somewhere folded ourselves up to build our nest
In a dark alley of life
You always remember
We have been troubled by your walking
But we have been delighted as well
By giving our present to your future
It's us on whose present stands your future

If you have any empathy for us
Then O wayfarer, midway somewhere before touching the horizon
Please do not stop
You only walk on, O wayfarer, you walk on

If you ever despair
And if you lose heart
Walking and walking alone on the path of life
When you do not get inspired
Do not lose heart
You consider this path as a stage
Think of yourself as only an actor
Who pretends to walk
Keep walking with the imagination of there
To reach where you started walking
Keep walking holding the rope of your breaths
When your feet turn heavy
Advance and go further
When it seems impossible, then you borrow
From your imagination, the twin wings of imagination
And fly away with their help towards the horizon
Where feet can not take you
The wings will take you
Yes there, reaching where you realize that imagination is reality
Yes reality, which seemed like imagination at first
You will know this reaching there
To reach where, O wayfarer, you are walking

Wherever your legs tire
Take the wings of imagination and fly ahead
Do not stop, you just walk on

Walking and walking when the evening sets in on your life
The desperation to reach your aim increases in your heart
And your legs tire
You do not be afraid with the encompassing night
That you would not be able to reach
You might think you could not do much
You did not get any pleasure anywhere
How would it have been if you had participated in crowd
Met someone who could have shared your heart
Eliminating pain, would have applied balm on your burning heart
O wayfarer, thinking this at the evening of life
Do not despair and don't you lose heart
You remember you set out to walk and so you walk
Do not care if the sun sets on your life on the path itself
Take some rest for a moment
Close your eyes for a moment
When the morning will arrive, the sun of life will shine again
O wayfarer, you rise with reserves of new life
Keeping the sight on horizon
With dream in your eyes of touching it
You walk again, keep walking
On the path of infinity, do not stop; walk on

Walking on the path of life
You will meet many who feign to walk
Trying to speak your language
But attention, O wayfarer
You do not be deceived by them
Who talk of walking
But are standing on the corner of a blind alley
They will call you in your language
But don't you listen to their shouts
You see their feet
See if they are pricked with thorns of path
See if there are calluses of toil
If not, then on hearing the talk that sounds your own
You smile and quietly advance
Because the one who walks
Is sure to get fatigued
And have hurt feet
You see that and move ahead
Stop not, to touch the horizon walk on

Before walking you may be afraid
Your heart might tremble, but it is only natural
All are scared of the unknown
They think how will they know
That, which they do not know
But with a dream in eyes of knowing that
What you do not know
But want to know some day
You just start walking and keep walking
It would be difficult to start, to take the first step
But you muster courage, take inspiration from your own dream
And take the first step
You will find that after starting nothing is really difficult
Go on taking steps one by one
Keep the dream in front of you and walk, walk after it
To touch the horizon, on the path of life, towards infinity you keep
walking

Walking and walking, remember, that moment will come
When walking will be natural and stopping will be difficult
And when that moment comes
Then you just thank yourself
Because it is you
Who is walking
With a dream in eyes of reaching there
To reach where
You had started and you are still walking
But until this happens, O wayfarer, you do not stop anywhere
Holding the hand of hope, you only keep walking

On the path of life when the evening of life sets it
Do not be afraid watching the darkness of death
You would surely be troubled
A little frightened may be, but do not let go of courage
You take inspiration from yourself
And with a dream in eyes of reaching there
Do not be afraid of darkness
Remember, you would have heard
When darkness comes, so does the moon
With the help of moonlight
Beyond the evening of life
When the darkness of death surrounds you
You only walk, do not stop
This moon will show you the way
On that path of life which you have taken
And it will help you till a new morning of life comes
With that waiting within
And the dream of reaching there in eyes
You keep walking, O wayfarer, do not stop
And do not lose heart, you just walk on

You started walking
With a dream in eyes of touching the horizon
Many stopped you
Who appeared to be your own
You met a crowd too
Speaking your language, to stop you
But you did not
With your own support and sometimes that of the wings of
imagination
You walked leaving the footprints in the passage of time
On the path of life with a trembling heart
And with the reserves of life, you walked
Don't you think
How important it was to start walking
If you do not realize this while walking
When you reach the horizon
And succeed in touching it
Then you look back
Because then only you can look without worry
Then you will not be afraid of stumbling
You would have found your horizon, and then you turn around and
see
You will find thousands are walking
Taking inspiration
From your own footprints
Then you would realize that the one who walks alone
Only he can inspire others
And is delighted to be an inspiration
But until you touch the horizon and become an inspiration
O wayfarer, do not stop anywhere
To touch the horizon you walk on

On the path of life with a dream of touching the horizon
Keeping the sight on horizon, taking the help of imagination
You walk and while walking you keep in mind
That you are looking towards infinity
Walking on that path of life
Which is stony and slippery

Beware, do not end up losing your sight in infinity
You anyway have to reach there
But you have to walk on this difficult path
Where, if you miss you will stumble and fall
The swamp of life will swallow you
Fallen, you can get injured
Remember this path, O wayfarer
You have walked on which as a wayfarer
With reserves of life
To touch your horizon, to know your perimeter you have walked

You remember
The sight can be on infinity, but you have to see the path too
Walk carefully
Even if you have to reduce speed
It is better to slow down and walk than to fall
O wayfarer! You be careful
To touch the horizon, to know your frontiers
You walk, do not stop, you walk on

You started walking on this difficult path of life
With a trembling heart
And wounds of inspiration in your heart
Which will ooze until you reach there,
To reach where you had started walking

Walking and walking your legs will tire
They will be wounded by the thorns of the way
Your only solace would be the dust strewn on the path
With blistered, heavy feet you keep walking
Make tiredness your own support
You only keep walking yourself

When it will be an end of your walking
You will reach there, yes that same horizon
That you had walked to touch
Then sit and see your dusty wounded feet
They were your companions of path
Which faced everything while traversing the path of life
And brought you here
To reach where you started walking
Sometime O wayfarer, you remember
To wash them with tears of joy that will flow
When you reach there, to reach where you had started walking.

When you would be walking towards infinity to see the infinite
By lightening the lamp of life, with the help of which
You will have to weather storms
And those frightful dark clouds
Which would want to stop your way before night sets in
And fill the flame of the lamp with darkness
You will think it is going to die soon
But do not be afraid; Fill the lamp of life with that
Which has oozed from your heart by the wounds of inspiration
As you fill the lamp with it
The brightness of hope and dreams will spread
It will remove the dark storm of the path
Which could have stopped you from walking
Taking this lamp, and brightness of hope in your heart
O wayfarer, you walk
Whether it is storm or anything else
You do not stop, you do not be afraid
Your lamp will not extinguish
As it is filled with effervescence of inspiration
And is giving the brightness of hope
Taking that in your heart
O wayfarer, you do not stop, you walk on.

While walking on the path you will meet despair
Yes, it will accompany you
It will be that companion
Whom, after reaching your goal
And touching the horizon, you will surely recognize
That it was only joy
Whom, fatigued by walking, you thought otherwise
It will walk with you wearing the clothes of despair
Accept it and drink it in the cup of toil
You will think of it as poison as first
But nectar of life it will be in result
You would know this, only when you reach there
To reach where you had started walking
You think of consequence
Do not stop O wayfarer, do not be afraid of despair
It in fact will prove to be the nectar of life
Which will wash all your grief
That you accumulated while walking on the path
But till such time as this happens, O wayfarer
Do not stop midway
To touch the horizon, you walk on

Walking and walking when you see that evening is setting
And the moonless night is surrounding with the darkness of death
Seeing it you will tremble wondering what will happen now
How would I walk; would I be able to see the horizon, my goal?
That for which, with dream in my heart
Holding the rope of breath, I had walked
What will happen now?
O wayfarer, if this happens in your path ever
Do not be afraid, do not lose hope
Light up that dark night with the experience you earned
Like a firefly that shines with its own light
You burn
And light up your path
Which you have to walk, and have been walking till now
Do not fear the darkness of death
Igniting your consciousness with experience
You light up yourself
O wayfarer, you advance, stop not
Before touching the horizon you walk on

Walking and walking on the path of life
When hope turns in to hopelessness
And dead tired you
Think you can not walk any further
Then do not stop
Be careful; do not let the lamp of hope extinguish
No one would help you even a little to light it up
Caught in the whirlwind of despair
You would not know if you can light it up again
You be awake, guard this lamp of hope
When you would steadfastly resolve to walk
You would hear a tired, feeble call of your heart
That stop not
The path that this is, you have to turn your blood in to water
And you have to leave every negative thought
If you can leave the despair, the hope will awaken
And it will become a youthful lass that will abide by you
Let your heart embrace her
And giving her your support
Only advance, do not stop, and walk on

Walking and walking your body
When becomes dead tired
Each and every step would feel
As if it is the last
O wayfarer, you do not be afraid and do not lose hope
You leave the company of hopelessness
And cling to hope
It will take you forward
That hope, which takes birth from your dream
That you saw before you started walking
Yes, that of touching the horizon
That of seeing your own perimeter
You do not stop, keep walking
Even if your body ever falls off walking and walking
And the fire of pyre burns it to ashes
Even then you do not be afraid
Yes, do not fear; your dreamy hope alone will become the wind
And will take your ashes to the horizon
It will scatter them there
To reach where you had started once
You do not fear and never lose hope
O wayfarer, to touch the horizon just walk on

Walking and walking on path of life
O wayfarer, if you are ever sad
Thinking of one you never wanted to leave
But walking was more important for you
So you walked, leaning on your dreams
To know your perimeter, you walked
The person you left behind must have been sad too
He wanted to bind you in his limits
But you did not bind
Because when one walks holding the companionship of hope
To touch the horizon, he does not stop
Does not get tied up in anyone's bondage
And does not even get limited in anyone's imposed limits
He only sets out
To know the unknown
Taking himself with him
And the one who was left behind, in memory of whom you are sad
O wayfarer, this sadness will weigh on your feet
See, you do not stop anywhere
Do not go back
Because the one who was sad due to your walking
And remained somewhere behind, limited in limits
You remember, he did not have dreams
He was looking away from the horizon
He did not have the desperation to know the unknown
That's why he remained, did not walk with you
Did not succeed even in stopping you
Do not be sad remembering him
If he was your companion, he would have been with you too
O wayfarer, do not be sad, reflect and advance
Do not stop you walk on

With the dream of touching the horizon
And to know your perimeter
O wayfarer, when you will start walking
And when you will cross
The hurdles that come with starting the walk
Then you will see a few footprints
That will be going far on this infinitely stretched path of life
Seeing them you will be surprised
Wondering how would they be
Who left before you to touch the horizon
Would they have reached?
These footprints will inspire you
You clench on to that ray of inspiration
And keep walking keeping your sight there,
Where meet the earth and the sky
Watching the footprints that will fade
You only advance
When you will reach that point
Where life and death embrace each other
There you will meet your horizon
You will see the perimeter too

Then you will see those who walked before you
Taking inspiration from their footprints, you walked too
There, where meet the life and the death
And become one
There you will find yourself
Seeing your own footprints you will be delighted too
But till then O wayfarer!
Holding the rope of inspiration, you just walk on

The journey from birth to death
This is the path of life
On which you have to walk O wayfarer, with the support of
breaths
And with the dream of knowing the death
It is this imagination which inspires you to walk
O wayfarer, when you walk, you just go on

It is this path on which knowingly or unknowingly everyone walks
But they fear the result
But you do not be afraid
What everyone thinks of as an end
You will find the beginning there; do not stop
Do not be lost in the narrow lanes on the path of life
You will find the path of life high and low often
But you do not stop
Your walking will level it
O wayfarer, with the cord of breaths
With the dream in eyes of seeing your perimeter
Lighting up the lamp of hope in heart
You only keep advancing, keep walking

Walking and walking on the path of life
You will find many thorns to make the passage difficult
And there will be pebbles scattered
When you will walk on the road of life
You will find all this
Walking and walking with your sight on the goal
Holding the rope of hope
What you had seen through dream
And you have set out to realize
You will find many hurdles
You can pass unscathed from them
Leaving the thorns and pebbles, you can leave now
But stop for a moment and think
Those who will watch your footprints
Even when you are not anymore
Those, who will take inspiration from your walking
You remember them
Don't you forget those too who will come behind you someday
You stop when you find the most difficult hurdle on the way
You stop and apply your might
A little apart from walking
To remove what you could escape
But, perhaps those who will come after you
Those who will watch your footprints
May be they will miss those footprints
And get hurt from the pebbles
And get pricked by thorns
You remove them

Walking and walking you keep removing those hurdles of the path
Walking and walking on the path of life
You widen the road for those who will come behind you
O wayfarer, you keep walking; do not stop
Only keep walking, removing the hurdles of the way, you keep
walking

When you will walk on the path of life, to know life itself
With dreams and curiosity in heart
Then, O wayfarer, you will find a few people
Whom you will find different from that crowd,
Which will preach you not to walk
Which will challenge you not to walk
Which will remind you of the duty not to walk
Duty, that is born out of frustration of not walking
And people glorify that frustration
By calling it duty

So the people, whom you would find different from the crowd
You be cautious, yes these are those
Who will lecture you on salvation and on finding the unmanifest,
By opening a shop somewhere
And calling it religion

You save yourself, you keep away from them
Because they will be more ferocious than the crowd
And yes, the crowd will be because of them
You do not get affected by their talk of salvation
They will say that to achieve your goals
Walking is not required
They will be worshipping the footprints of someone, presuming
him to be a messiah
You see in their eyes
You will find only an extreme anxiety
There will be a hidden wail in their being

You listen to them, after listening you move ahead
If they could have walked to achieve the goal of life
You would not have found them in the crowd increasing the crowd
further
You would have found only a few footprints
Seeing them, you just go straight ahead
O wayfarer, do not stop; to touch the horizon, you walk on

Facing the blows of life, swallowing your tears
Sitting in the fantasy of achieving something
Think about your desperation
Think of you being paused, sitting wrapped in a place
In a circle drawn by yourself
Would you achieve anything, would you reach anywhere?
Think, would you be able to accept this?
Would you bear this naked truth
That if you do not walk, you would not reach anywhere
You will only become the dust of the path
And a part of that crowd
Which you see stopping the way of those who walk
Would you be happy? Think, and dream of there
Someplace where, meet life and death
You try to bring the yearning inside you
To touch that same horizon
You get up wayfarer, and only walk
Leaning on the dream
Lighting up the lamp of hope in heart
To touch the horizon you begin the course of walking
From wherever you walk, that will be your beginning
But see, after walking a while you will find
You had set out a long ago
Realized only now, you were not sitting but walking
When you realize this, then you look ahead
And with the zest of walking inside you
Only keep walking
Do not stop; to touch the horizon keep walking

Walking on the path of life
You had set out on which O wayfarer
If you do not find any footprints on the path
Which could have inspired you to walk
Do not be worried
If you do not find the dust of time on the path
Which can take imprints of feet
You turn around and see from where you are standing
And then see the horizon ahead at once
You will find the horizon alone will attract you
When that attraction awakens in your heart
Then you dream of touching the horizon

Think, reaching there you would be able to see your own perimeter
And then just walk, do not care
That there are no footprints of anyone to inspire you
You be your own inspiration
Taking dreams as companions
Just walk

When you move ahead
And examine yourself, walking and walking
You will pass that, leaving your footprints
Which will someday be called the path of those coming behind you
Which many will walk, taking inspiration from your footprints
Then you will be called the maker of that path
Till then you walk, to touch your own perimeter
Leaving your own footprints, walk on

When you will walk on the path of life
To know yourself and to touch the horizon
Taking hope filled with dreams, leaning on yourself when you will walk
Whirlwinds, do not know how many, will grow inside you
Emotions, do not know how many, will rise within you

O wayfarer, you endure the pains that will come
When the thorns of this path prick you, you endure them
Stop those which flow from eyes
Bite your lips, seal them
Do not let out a sigh from within
O wayfarer, you endure
All this, one has to bear, he who walks
On this path to know the life
Do not cry; endure the difficulties of this path of life
Which you will feel you can not surmount

But you clasp tightly that dreamy hope
To touch that, yes that same unknown horizon
To touch which you have walked
Do not stop till then, until you know that for which you have
walked
O wayfarer, do not stop you only walk

When you will start walking O wayfarer
Then those who will stop you but will not be able to stop
Will not succeed in stopping your departure
Then it is possible that they will blame you
A feeling of smallness will arise within those
Who could not walk, because they lacked the courage to walk
They will call you a fugitive and will call you so many names
Which you would not have been able to take
Had you not seen the horizon
If you had not set out to touch the horizon

O wayfarer, you endure their arrows
They will say that you are full of inadequacies
You do not have a single quality
If you had some, you would have nestled
And would have remained within those limits
In which remain all and become dust
They remain there because they are afraid of walking
They fear therefore they stop you
You, O wayfarer, but listen to everything
And walk, saying to them
My walking has no quality
Hey you, who stop me by calling me your own
Agreed, I have no qualities, and
You will forget all my inadequacies
Once I am not there in front of you
But now I have to walk
Have to reach very far
Shall I leave now? Saying this O wayfarer, you just move ahead
Do not stop, keep on walking

When you walk breaking all the ties
Forgetting all the qualities and inadequacies
When you walk on that difficult path
Holding the rope of inspiration
With hope in heart
When you just walk to touch the horizon
Crossing all the hurdles

Then your remember
When they would not succeed in stopping you
And you would have come some distance
The world will call you cheerfully
You will hear words of praise coming from far
O wayfarer, you will hear them, and it will feel very good
somewhere inside
You would want to stop and listen to those sweet words of praise

But be forewarned, dismiss them after hearing
It will be that last hurdle
Which if entices you, you would not walk again
You will stop walking after a few steps
O wayfarer, you remember this, do not listen
You keep sight there, where meet life and death
And just walk holding the rope of inspiration
And carrying hope within
To touch the horizon, you walk on

Leaving your nestle, O wayfarer, taking wings of imagination
Keeping the dream ahead
To touch the sky, you fly leaving behind your pain

In that firmament you will feel you are getting lost
You are not getting any direction
Where you could have touched the sky
But you fly taking the wings from imagination
O wayfarer, to touch the infinite you fly
This flight itself will rest
Your injured tired legs
O wayfarer, you fly; flying and flying when you become still
In the flight of imagination itself
Then you will find immensity in front of you

The horizon too will become as vast
As high as you fly taking wings of imagination
Your confidence will go up as much
As high as you fly
When you accept the challenge
To touch the limit of infinity yourself
Then you would not be able to stop

Fast and faster, high and higher you would keep flying
Taking support from wings of imagination you would fly
When you would have rested for a moment
Your injured tired legs
O wayfarer, then you climb down to the ground of reality
And move ahead
Do not stop, just walk on

People see the moon
Getting attracted to its beauty
In that dark night when it shows the path
Spreading its moonlight
Those who walk sustained by that moonlight
Just walk ahead and those who do not want to walk
May be they never wanted to walk
They look for blemishes on the face of moon
Forgetting its moonlight
Yes that same moonlight which enabled them to see those
blemishes
If the moon did not show those blemishes itself
Would they have seen?

Many say that its moonlight is not something it earned
It has taken it from sun; does it have anything of its own?
Just viewing, they see only blemishes
But those who walk supported by the moonlight
On the path in that dark night
They know that even if moon did not earn the light itself
But still for those who walk, it is at least reflecting the light
Keeping away the fear of exposing blemishes
So that someone walks, he who wanted to walk
But would have been lost in darkness
For him alone it is reflecting the light
Exposing all its shortcomings
It is showing the way

O wayfarer, you thank him,
Whose moonlight supports you to walk in this darkness
Thanking him, who would disappear beyond the horizon,
After showing you the way in darkness
O wayfarer, you remember him,
The one who has showed you the way in darkness
Spreading his moonlight
He, who did not hide his blemishes
To show the way to him, who is walking on this path of life
O wayfarer, you salute him silently and move ahead
Your walking will make his moonlight meaningful
Which he reflected
To show the way in darkness
To him who will walk
O wayfarer, you walk, to touch the horizon you just walk on

When you walk you remember this
It would not matter
What all you endure, walking on the path of life

In choosing your goal, you will endure tears, stumbles,
And illusions of happiness
You shall endure
Enduring all this, think, O wayfarer
You think.

What?

It all does not end
Without leaving a mark
But the one who, walking on this difficult path of life
Pours out his heart
On a few leaves of paper
And moves ahead on the path of life
Yes, on that same difficult path
Is certain to leave his footprints

When you will leave footprints, O wayfarer,
Then probably you would understand
That real significance of life lies
In leaving the footprints

Only after leaving the footprints, this you would understand
O wayfarer, do not forget, leaving footprints on the difficult path
of life
You only keep walking, do not stop; just walk on

O wayfarer, when you will see the dream
Of touching the horizon,
Of reaching there, where life and death appear to meet
When you set out to realize that dream of yours
When you will walk and move ahead
Then you will understand how to walk

Walking on the path of life
You will see beauty scattered everywhere
Crossing the hurdles of path
You will also see the beauty of hurdles
That comes to the fore when you cross them

Then you will remember that crowd
Which you met
When you had taken only a few steps
You had only started walking
Carrying that dreamy hope within when you walked
When you will remember, you will feel at once
That call I should; I should call that crowd too
Compassion will arise within you
For that, which stopped
For that, which wanted you to merge in it
It frightened, it taunted
But could not stop you
Walking was more important to you than stopping
You could not stop; you had to walk so you walked

Remembering that crowd you would think, should I call?
So that they could see this scattered beauty too
So that they could see this horizon too
But, O wayfarer, you stop and think
If you think, you will understand
That the crowd does not have ears
That could make it hear someone's call
It probably does not have eyes either
That could make it see the beauty of life
You think; you do not call
Move ahead leaving footprints
Which would inspire the one who wants to walk
He will walk indeed without worrying about the crowd
O wayfarer, you walk; do not stop, keep walking

If you fall in the mud of life, O wayfarer,
And when you feel
You would not be able to wash this dirt
That has tainted you
Walking on the path of life
You do not be sad
Don't you be sad that you are covered with mud
And there is nothing you could wash with
Or clean yourself with
Do not be sad
Even after falling in this mud,
In which fall many
And remain lost there, hating themselves
You do not be like them
When you are not able to remove it
Making this mud your support
In which you have fallen
Yes, making this mud your support, O wayfarer,
You set roots in it
And becoming a lotus, blossom

Rise above the mud filled limits of life
Becoming lotus you will find a new road
Then you would not be able to stop, you will only walk
But this walking will be different this time
You will walk, carrying the scent of lotus this time
By transforming the mud in scented beauty
You will walk to touch the horizon
Leaving behind that mud
Because of which you could become a lotus
O wayfarer, only walk ahead, do not stop, keep walking
Becoming a lotus from mud, you keep walking

When the consciousness will awaken in you
You will find that whoever has materialized
Remains somewhere in the stream of time
Holding anything, just anything
To keep his existence
He clings to anything

O wayfarer, when the consciousness will awaken in you
You will find that you are also holding something
And will understand that holding something
Becomes the way of life for everyone
Those who remain in the stream of time holding something
To keep their existence
Do they save their existence by doing this?
You leave whatever you have been holding since birth
You leave that
Let go of yourself in the stream of time
Staying in which makes you not see it
Though it keeps flowing
To touch that unknown horizon
You also flow with it
Do not hold anything
You let go and just flow

Flowing, it will take you along
There, to reach where you have been dreaming
Let go; then do not hold anything
And flow ahead flowing in the stream of time
You will find that life is nothing
Apart from time

Just a bubble of time it is
Flowing in the stream of time
You do not fear; only keep flowing
If the bubble of your life bursts
Even then you do not fear
You will understand while flowing
That when the bubble of your life bursts
Only then shall you become one with that
What you have been flowing in

Do not hold anything, leave everything
And flow in the stream of time

The feelings of your heart
Which remain hidden somewhere in that depth
To understand it, to measure that depth
Yes, that same depth which is in us all
But seems as if it is nowhere
Not sure whether it is even there or not

You plunge inside your heart
And select those shining pearls of feelings hidden in it
Bring them and spread them on the path of life
Which only you can bring
Climbing down in your heart
O wayfarer, you dive deep, do not fear
Until you find them
Walking on the path of life
From the depth of your heart
Select those,
Yes, those pearls, the craving and desperation of acquiring those
Will give you an inspiration to dive
Till you do not get that, O wayfarer,
You do not stop and you do not lose heart
Taking the treasure of breaths and inspiration in heart
You dive yourself in your own depth
And hunt for that feeling
Yes, that same feeling, which will take you to that side of horizon

Till such time as you find it
O wayfarer, do not lose courage
Holding the rope of inspiration
Take the plunge, bring that out O wayfarer
Taking that, yes that, you walk ahead
Do not stop, only keep walking

When you will walk on the path of life
Enduring the pricking of thorns strewn on the path
Carrying the dream within of touching the horizon
When you will walk
You will endure what not
Probably that, which they call sorrow

Those who do not walk fearing the difficulty of path
Remain somewhere in the imagination of happiness limiting
themselves
Those who remain, they will say why take pains
What is there in walking?
There, in knowing that unknown
You will get only thorns and stumbles in life
You stay here with us
Making a nest of yours

O wayfarer, you listen to everything
Endure the pricking of thorns strewn on the path
Endure stumbles that one always has to endure
Who walks on the difficult path of touching that horizon

You endure all the pains
Which those who do not walk call sorrow
Wherever, whenever you will touch your horizon
And will go beyond it
Then the satisfaction that you will get
By realizing your dream
Whatever you have endured for that
Will you be able to remember that?

O wayfarer, you will plunge in the ecstasy of touching the horizon
But until this happens, fearing the sorrow
And the pricking of thorns
O wayfarer, you do not stop
To touch the horizon you walk on

Extolling walking as great and declaring themselves as the ones
who walk
On the path, are many, who live in a pleasant fantasy
That does not take anywhere
But gives them a pleasant illusion, that of walking on the path
They think of themselves as owners of an emotional heart
Despite being heartless they talk of making the path easy

But this thought of theirs is only as deep
As thin their skin is
They only want to impress
That crowd which wants to stop
The one who walks quietly to touch the horizon
Carrying the dream in eyes of knowing one's perimeter
He walks quietly
No one is able to stop him
And he does not talk about widening the road
He only sets out
Carrying silent inspiration in heart
Holding the rope of breaths
Following that dreamy hope
Which takes him to the horizon

And those who nurture the pleasant illusion of walking on their path
To impress that crowd
Which stops those who walk
You do not become like them
O wayfarer, you remember
Do not nurture the illusion of walking
Do not consider yourself more emotional than others

It is this illusion that stops everyone from walking
You only start walking
Carrying dream in eyes
To touch the horizon, you start walking
Just start walking, do not stop; keep walking

Walking on the path of life
O wayfarer, if you turn in to a blind alley
Which may seem tempting at first
But traps you in darkness

Yes, if you get trapped
In such a blind alley, in its darkness
And when you are not able to see
The horizon and you yourself
Then you remember
Many remained trapped here in the imagination of pleasure
Nurturing many illusions of making a nest
That imagination which could only give them an illusion of
pleasure
And made them dust
Giving many hopes, it did not let them see the horizon
Trapping them in the darkness of life
Do not forget, after getting used to the darkness
Light hurts
O wayfarer, you always remember this
And do not fear what will happen now
Before you get used to the darkness
And start getting afraid of opening your eyes
You come back
You come back; do not stop even out of compassion
For those who are trapped in the darkness of some dark alley
You come back there
From where you can see the horizon
From there carrying the dream in eyes
To touch that, you start walking towards it
To know your perimeter, you just start walking
Do not stop till you touch the horizon, just keep walking

When you walk on the path of life, O wayfarer
Carrying dream in eyes of touching the horizon
With a trembling heart and a hope within
O wayfarer, when you start walking
It may happen that in your innocent enthusiasm
You are tricked by somebody's sweet talk
Which is spoken to stop those
Who walk to touch the horizon
When you are trapped by the voice that sounds intimate
In the blind alleys found on the path of life
And when you recover to feel that you are too late
And doubts start breeding within you
Whether you would be able to walk or not
You will experience anger filled frustration too
Anger which will be born out of frustration of stopping
You might come to hate that intimate speech
Which has trapped you on some blind turning of life
You will also blame it a lot

But beware O wayfarer, if you have understood that you were trapped
You would be surrounded by doubt
Whether you would be able to walk or not
You remain forewarned, just see the horizon once and start walking
Do not stop to blame anyone in angry frustration
In blaming, many have lost their present
In losing their present they have lost their future too
Be not like them

Taking a deep breath and the experience of getting trapped
Just seeing the horizon, you walk ahead
Do not stop and do not blame anyone
If you start walking, where will you find the time
To blame anyone
You just start walking towards the horizon
By supporting yourself
You move ahead, do not stop; just walk on

Walking and walking on the path of life
If you find someone who can walk, accompanying you
Taking inspiration from your dream, he sets out to touch the
horizon
Leaving everything behind
With a trembling heart and the pleasure in heart of walking with you

Getting inspired from your dream
If you find someone accompanying you
Then take his hand in yours
O wayfarer, watching the infinity, advance to touch the horizon
Taking his support you keep walking
To touch the horizon keep walking
Walking and walking if somewhere your companion wears out
And moving ahead, walking ahead becomes impossible for him
with his injured legs
When his weariness obstructs your advance
And you, trapped in attachment,
Want to stop to accompany him
That will only be natural
Because the friendship that comes by walking some distance
Ties you in the bond of attachment
O wayfarer, you beware
Leaving his hand
Seeing your companion with eyes full of compassion
Taking a cold breath you move ahead
Do not be trapped in attachment
Because you have to reach all the way up to the horizon
If you stop to support, you would not be able to walk again
Say to your companion - you rest for a moment

Then you walk, you will find me waiting at the horizon
There, I will welcome you
You come after taking some rest
There on the horizon we shall meet
You do not stop, you come over
Saying this O wayfarer, you start walking ahead
Do not stop, just start walking
To touch the horizon, keep walking on

When you walk leaving attachment behind, and all ties of
compassion
When even the crowd is not able to stop you
Leaving even the ties of friendship
When you walk on the path of life
Carrying dream in eyes and inspiration within
O wayfarer, when they would not succeed in stopping you
Then those, who at first seemed very much your own
You would have to hear much from them that could hurt you
It will pierce you from within
You will get blames do not know how many
You endure them
It will be very difficult
But endure the injuries of speech that will hit you; that you have to
hear
Because you have set out to touch the horizon
To know your perimeter
Your waking on would have frustrated them from within
Their envy will come out
In the form of bitter speech clad in anger, to hurt you
You endure that quietly and remain cautious of them
Do not hate those who utter words
To diminish your enthusiasm
You do not hate, you save yourself from it
For this will be the tie, strongest of them all
To escape from it would be a little difficult
You do not get tied in the strings of hate
You be cautious
Many ended up becoming the dust on the path
They, who could escape even the ties of friendship

The crowd could not stop them
Even they, while walking, got tied up in the strings of hate
Only to become the dust of path
O wayfarer, you escape from that, be cautious
Do not look away from the horizon, do not consider anyone enemy
Do not hate anyone
Endure everything quietly
Carrying only the dream in eyes and the inspiration within
You move ahead
To touch the horizon, just walk on

Walking on the path of life
Enduring the pricking of thorns strewn on the path
Stopping those which flow from eyes
Sealing your lips, admiring the beauty of thorns that never wither
Escaping the hurdles that stop the way
When you advance
Experiencing the emotions in life
To touch the horizon, carrying the sentiment within of touching
the horizon
And carrying the dream in eyes while watching the infinity
Where life and death appear to meet
When you would be walking on the path of life
The difficulty of which makes many bite the dust
Leaving footprints on that dust, when you would be walking on the
path of life
Experiencing the emotions in their entirety
Then you would understand sometime while walking on the path
That those who lack feelings
They murder
The delicate emotions rising within someone
Stomping the delicate emotions is the medium of entertainment of
those
Who lack feelings
O wayfarer, do not become like them
While walking on the path of life

This cruelty is born out of the frustration of not walking
You escape from it, respect each of those delicate sentiments
Which rises within him
Who is able to see the horizon and dreams of touching it
O wayfarer, saving yourself from the murderers of sentiments
You just move ahead on the path of life
Keep walking and walking; before you touch the horizon
Do not stop, just walk on

Walking on the path of life
To touch the horizon, with a trembling heart
And a shivering within to know the unknown
O wayfarer, when you will walk, you will see
What they call humanity, yes that term humanity
Hearing the praise and song of which, O wayfarer, you have been
walking
To know life and death

You will understand while walking on the path of life
That none is crueler than humans in this creation
Who could show more cruelty than humans for their kin
Yes, it is only a human being who in the name of humanity
Does what is inhuman
You will understand, whatever is called inhuman
Is done by none other than a human being
You will see whatever is inhuman
Is done by a human being alone
Animals will appear better than humans to you
Because they kill to fill their stomach
And a human being, he kills only to prove
His superiority to other humans
He is not compassionate to other humans

O wayfarer, seeing this you will fear
Your heart will tremble
You might be repentant
About being a human
But you do not lose heart, don't you lose heart

As a human seeing the cruelty of other humans
Walking on the path of life
You show them your humane side
Show them that a human can leave cruelty and be sensitive
He can shed a tear or two watching someone in pain
That someone can set out on the path of life to know himself
To touch the horizon; to know the limits of self

O wayfarer, you become human in real terms
To touch the horizon only keep walking

Time does not have a feeling
But every feeling has its own time
You will understand, O wayfarer, that
While walking on the path of life
What you were thinking of as life
Was nothing but time

But you would understand this only after reaching the horizon
After touching it there, where life and death appear to meet
Attracted by the beauty of this union
You had walked taking inspiration from your dream
With a trembling heart, after that dreamy hope
That took you here, where you are standing after getting your
horizon

Knowing your limits, you have known
That there is nothing other than time
Time has produced everything, the path and you yourself too
Living in the stream of time, leaning on time
Under the illusion of holding something, to save their own
existence
Many were lost in time
No sign remained of them
Who wanted to save just their own existence

O wayfarer, you left everything
Because to touch the horizon
To know the love between life and death
Was more important to you
Than to save the existence
You walked, you let yourself flow in the stream of time

Leaving your signs, somewhere in time
You flowed, reached the horizon
That is why you could know the existence of time
Your life was itself just a bubble of time
Which flowed in the stream of time
After getting your horizon, the bubble of your life has burst
And after knowing time you have become one with time
O wayfarer, you have made your walk meaningful
You walked, did not stop anywhere before touching the horizon
You only kept walking

When you will start knowing this light
You will understand that by knowing light
Begins the knowing of time
You will be able to understand that after crossing the limit of light
Begins the submerging in the limit of unlimited
You will understand this when you will know the light
Light, yes that same light which enables us to see the path
You can see the footprints left behind on the dust strewn on the
path
Of those who went ahead
With the help of this same light
Which everyone can see

Everyone tries to hold on
Because they are afraid of darkness
While trying to know the light, you will understand
Those who fear the darkness also fear the light
The intensity of its brightness closes their eyes
You do not shut them, keep them open
Do not shut your eyes, for if you get scared of light
You will be drowned in darkness
Sunken in darkness you would not be able to walk again
You would neither be able to see the path
Nor the footprints left behind by those who had walked ahead
Which could have inspired you
You will remain in darkness
You do not fear light
Do not close the eyes, bedazzled by its brilliance
You remember this while bearing its intensity
You keep the eyes open

Then you will understand, when you go beyond the intensity of its
brilliance
And know the light, you will know
That the beginning of knowing the time
Starts with knowing the light
This is that frontier, crossing which
The one who crosses gets submerged in the infinite
He is able to know the time
You do not stop and do not lose heart
When your eyes start getting bedazzled
And are filled with tears watching the intensity of its brilliance
Then you muster some courage
And keep flowing on the path of life
Do not stop O wayfarer, only keep walking

The horizon seeing which you are walking
It is only that limit of your vision
Beyond which you are not able to see
You are afraid of raising your sight perhaps
But by touching this frontier
You will be able to break a bond of you limitedness
When you will cross one frontier, then only you would understand
That after crossing one frontier
Begins the next immense frontier
You keep crossing the frontiers one by one
You search the new horizons for yourself
As many horizons you will cross that much immense you will
become
Do not stop at any frontier
Do not be afraid of any frontier
You only muster a little bit of courage within
And with dream in eyes
Keep advancing, to touch the horizon just keep walking on.

I had started walking
On the path of imagination
Imagining happiness
That perhaps I would reach my destination

But while walking
I took a detour
And reached
In the pursuit of happiness
A stony pathway
That only had scorching sun
And howling winds

Lost on the way
I kept walking for long
Kept walking, thinking perhaps
I would reach my destination
I would get some happiness
Even if only a little

Walking and walking
I was tired
And it was not possible to walk any further
Whatever I had gotten until now
Was anything but happiness
I was dead tired
I sat on the heap of those stones
Walking on which my feet had gone sore
The scorching sun and the gusty wind
Was blistering my skin
There, closing my eyes
I waited for death to come

After incessant crying
Even tears had left me
I was sitting on stones
With stony lonely eyes
My only friends were the adversities
They were the only ones
Who had not left me

All of a sudden, someone called me
"Is that all?
Would you come with me?
This is not the end of your world
This is not the moment to be tired and to stop walking
The walk really starts from now on
Come I will take you on the right path"

I could not believe
That even on this turn
Someone could come to support
Stumbling had become such a habit
That it had become my destiny

I was frightened by the kinship of the voice
I found it strange
Perhaps I had accepted the jabs of stony ways
As my companions

Then he said again
"Come with me
And tell me about your pain
Walking with you
I will share your burdens
I will remove your stifling sorrow
And I will remove those pains
Which you have deemed your companions

You come with me
On that pleasant path
Where you have to go
These are not the stony ways
They take you through breaths
To the depths of heart"

- Devahuti

Made in the USA
Monee, IL
25 September 2020